Let's Create with Paint

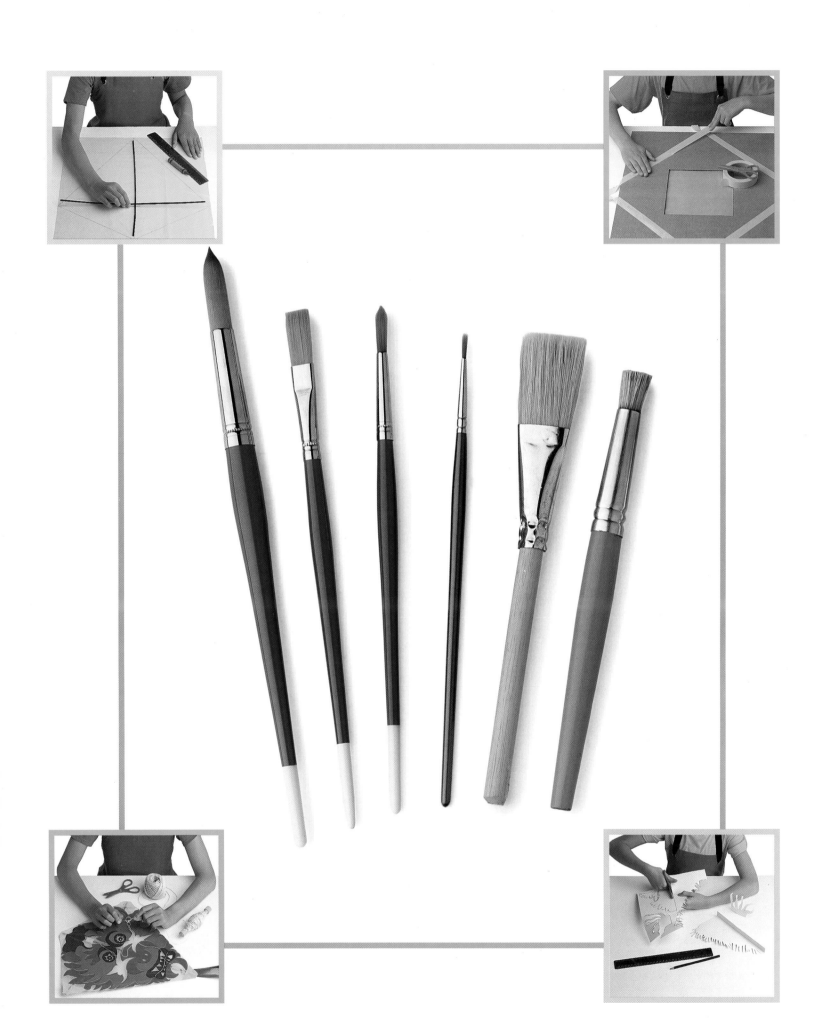

Let's Create
with Paint

DAWN SIRETT, ANGELA WILKES,
and
HELEN DREW

How to use this book

Let's Create With Paint shows you how to make and paint all kinds of wonderful things using everyday materials. Below are the points to look for on each page when using this book, and a list of things to remember.

Equipment

Illustrated checklists show you which tools to have ready before you start each project.

The things you need

The items for each project are clearly shown to help you check that you have everything you need.

Step-by-step

Step-by-step photographs and clear instructions tell you exactly what to do at each stage of a project.

Things to remember

- Read through all the instructions before you begin a project and gather together everything you will need.

- Put on an apron or an old shirt and roll up your sleeves before you start.

- Lay down lots of newspaper to protect worktables and the floor.

- Be very careful when using scissors or sharp knives. Do not use them unless an adult is there to help you.

- Always open the windows when using glaze* and ask an adult to clean the brush in turpentine for you.

- Put everything away when you have finished and clean up any mess.

We have used oil-based glaze for the projects in this book.

A DK PUBLISHING BOOK

Editor Sarah Johnston
Designers Caroline Potts and Adrienne Hutchinson
DTP Designer Almudena Díaz
Managing Editor Jane Yorke
Managing Art Editor Chris Scollen
US Editor Kristin Ward
Production Ben Smith
Photography Dave King
First American Edition, 1997
2 4 6 8 10 9 7 5 3 1
Published in the United States by DK Publishing Inc.,
95 Madison Avenue, New York, New York 10016
Visit us on the World Wide Web at http://www.dk.com

Copyright © 1997 Dorling Kindersley Limited, London
Projects originally published in *My First Activity Book, My First Paint Book,*
and *My First Music Book* Copyright © 1996, 1994, and 1993
Dorling Kindersley Limited, London

A catalog record for this book is available from the Library of Congress.

ISBN 0-7894-1559-3

Color reproduction by Colourscan
Printed and bound in Italy by L.E.G.O.

CONTENTS

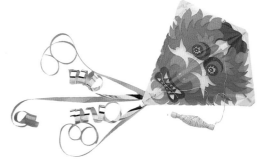

STENCIL DESIGNS

Stenciling is a fun way to repeat a picture or pattern. A stencil is a piece of cardboard with shapes cut out of it. To stencil, you hold the cardboard flat on a surface and paint through the holes. You can stencil on walls, furniture, or fabrics, but check with an adult first. Below, a palette and border of squares are stenciled on an art box. You can make up a picture or pattern to stencil. Always leave some cardboard around your designs and glaze the stencils to make them long-lasting. Practice using your stencils on scrap paper. You will need thick poster or acrylic paints and a stencil brush or sponge to paint with.

*Sponge**

EQUIPMENT

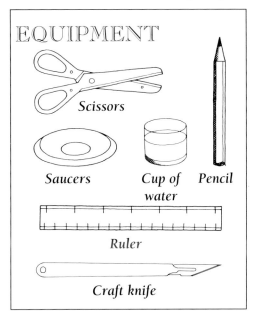

Scissors

Saucers   **Cup of water**   **Pencil**

Ruler

Craft knife

You will need

Clear glaze

Paintbrush for glazing the stencils

Stencil brush (or a brush with short, stiff hairs)

Poster paints (or you can use acrylic paints)

Making the box

1 Cut two pieces of cardboard to fit the length of the box. Make them twice the depth of the box and fold them in half as shown.

2 Paint or cover two matchboxes. Cut a length of cardboard to go across the box.** Make it twice the depth and fold it in half, as before.

3 Cut a slit halfway down one long partition and another halfway up the short partition so that they slot together as shown.

*Cut a small, thin piece from a household sponge.

**The cardboard should fit across the box from one side to the matchboxes, as shown.

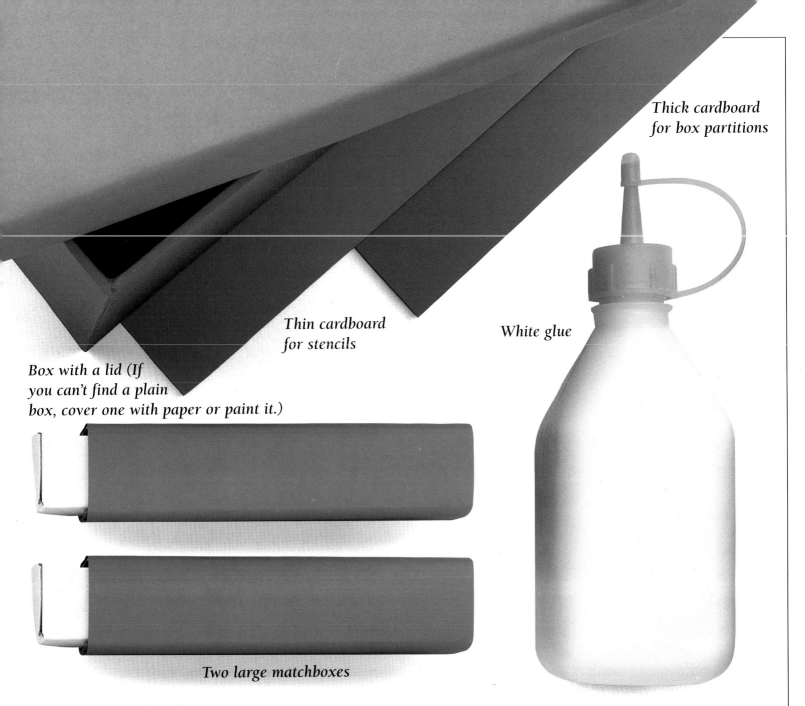

*Thick cardboard
for box partitions*

*Thin cardboard
for stencils*

White glue

*Box with a lid (If
you can't find a plain
box, cover one with paper or paint it.)*

Two large matchboxes

Stenciling the box

1. Draw a pattern or picture on a piece of cardboard. Ask an adult to cut out your design. Glaze both sides and leave it to dry.

2. Decide where you want your design to go on the box. Hold the stencil flat.* Paint in the holes with a stencil brush or sponge.

3. You can use more than one stencil to make a picture or pattern. Wait for the first color to dry before stenciling over it.

If you find it hard to hold the stencil in place, tape it down with masking tape.

7

STENCILED ART BOX

Your stenciled design can be repeated on each side of the art box, on the lid, and on the matchboxes, too. You can fill the box with all kinds of painting and drawing equipment. The bigger compartments can hold paintbrushes, paints, and pencils. The matchboxes are perfect for paper clips, erasers, or crayons. You might have room for other items, such as scissors and a roller, sponges, modeling tools, modeling clay, and glaze. The box could also be used to store jewelry, sewing equipment, or a collection.

Matchboxes make small compartments. Use as many as you need.

The three partitions divide the box into large and small compartments, which can hold different-sized objects.

A PLACE FOR EVERYTHING

Before you cut out your partitions, put everything you want the art box to hold into the box. This will help you figure out the best way to divide up your box.

STENCILING TIPS
• You may find it easier to paint the outside edge of the stencil hole first and work inward.
• To avoid smudging the paint, don't remove the stencil until the paint is dry.
• Use thick, sticky paint so that it doesn't run under the stencil.

The line of small red and yellow squares makes a decorative border.

Simple shapes work well when stenciled, such as these squares.

Colorful artist's palette design

PAINTING THEME

Two stencils were used for the palette design. First, the palette was stenciled in white and left to dry. Then the second stencil was held over the palette and the blobs of paint and brush were stenciled on top.

White palette stenciled first

Paints and brush stenciled over palette

Border of squares

9

A Diamond Kite

Make, paint, and fly a colorful kite with a wonderful dragon-face design! The kite is made from a large plastic bag. Look for a bag without any writing on it, such as a large garbage bag. Acrylic paints work best on plastic. If you don't have these, you can mix some white glue with poster paint, but you may find that some of the paint peels off the plastic.

Plant stakes are used for the kite spars. They make a frame for the plastic. Medium-sized stakes 18 in (46 cm) long should be the correct size. If they are too long, ask an adult to trim them.

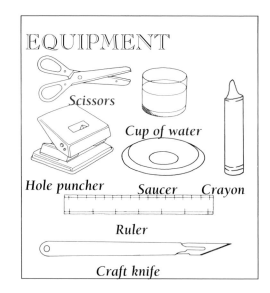

EQUIPMENT

Scissors

Cup of water

Hole puncher   Saucer   Crayon

Ruler

Craft knife

You will need

Strong plastic tape

Thin paintbrush

Medium paintbrush

Small stick

About 3 ft (90 cm) of strong thread

Large ball of string

Gift ribbon

Acrylic paints

Plant stakes

Large plastic bag

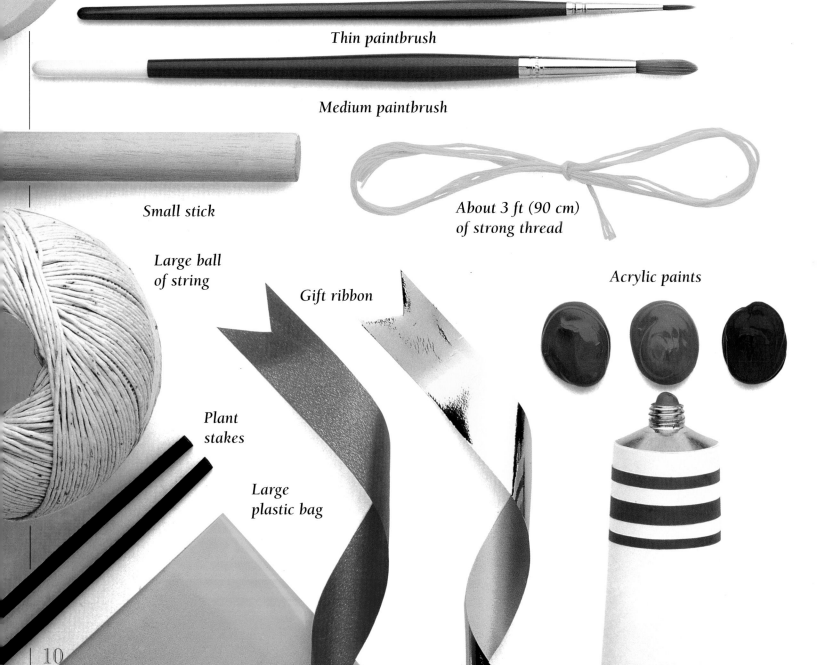

Making the kite

1 Cut out a 19-in (48-cm) square from a bag. Make three marks 5½ in (14 cm) down from the top, and three along center as shown.*

2 Join the marks on the edge of the plastic. Check that the plastic is ½ in (1 cm) bigger than the stakes all around. Cut out kite.

3 Stick tape on the kite's corners and also front and back on the center line 4 in (11 cm) from top, and 3 in (7 cm) from the bottom.

4 Fold each corner and punch through the folds to make two holes in each corner. Ask an adult to cut two slits on the center line.**

5 Paint a design on the kite and leave it to dry. Cut long lengths of gift ribbon. Hold them together and punch a hole in one end.

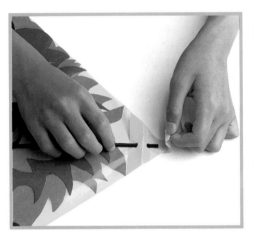

6 Turn the kite over. Thread one stake through the holes across the kite, as shown. Wrap tape over each end to hold the stake in.

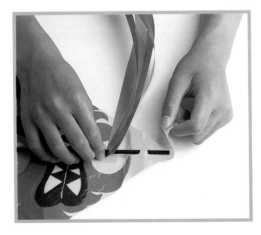

7 Thread the ribbons onto the other stake. Push it into top and bottom holes, and under the first stake. Tape over stake ends.

8 Turn the kite over. Push the ends of the thread through the slits in the kite's center and tie them to the upright stake at back.

9 Tie a small loop in the thread. It should be at a right angle to the kite, as shown. This is the kite's bridle.

*Fold the plastic in half to find the center.

** Cut the slits through the tape pieces you placed on the center line in step 3.

FLYING DRAGON

Attaching the string

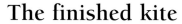

1 Wrap tape around each end of a small stick. Tie one end of a large ball of string to the stick and wind on about 100 ft (30 m).

2 When you are ready to fly your kite, tie the end of the string to the loop in the bridle. Knot it two or three times.

LAUNCHING THE KITE

When you want to fly your kite, make sure the string is tied securely to the bridle and stick. Find an open space. Unwind a little string. On a windy day, the kite should fly from your outstretched arm, or you can ask a friend to hold the kite at a distance and let go when it fills with wind. Once your kite is up, slowly let out more string.

Pull on the string and watch your kite rise up into the air!

The finished kite

You can copy this face or paint a different face on your kite; try an octopus, a lion, or a monster.

DOS AND DON'TS

• Never fly your kite in strong winds or stormy weather.
• Never fly near overhead cables, roads, cars, buildings, trees, people, animals, or an airport.
• Always wear gloves when kite-flying.
• Never look directly at the sun and always wear sunglasses to protect your eyes.

Stand with your back to the wind and hold the stick at each end.

If your kite doesn't fly very well, try adjusting the angle of the loop in the bridle.

A long tail looks spectacular and keeps your kite steady. Red and gold ribbons suggest fire coming from the dragon's mouth.

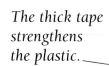

The thick tape strengthens the plastic.

The ends of the thread
are pushed through the
slits and tied to the
upright spar.

Make sure that the kite
spars lie on the side of the kite
that isn't painted and that they
hold the plastic fairly taut.

13

TINKLING TAMBOURINES

For hundreds of years, dancers and singers have been shaking brightly colored tambourines in time to music. Below you can find out how to make two tambourines from papier-mâché. You will need to leave the tambourines to dry for two or three days before you can paint them. If you turn the page, you can see the finished instruments and how to decorate them.

You will need

6½ ft (2 m) of colored ribbon

Poster paints

Clear glaze

Embroidery thread

A wooden skewer

EQUIPMENT

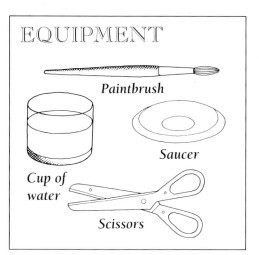

Paintbrush

Saucer

Cup of water

Scissors

Bell tambourine

1 Spread petroleum jelly thickly over the outside of the baking ring. Tear sheets of newspaper into small, rectangular pieces.

2 Stick pieces of newspaper to the ring with paste. Make sure that the pieces overlap each other so that there are no gaps left.

3 Build up layers of paper until the paper ring is ¼ in (0.5 cm) thick. Let the paper dry for three days, then slide it off the ring.

14

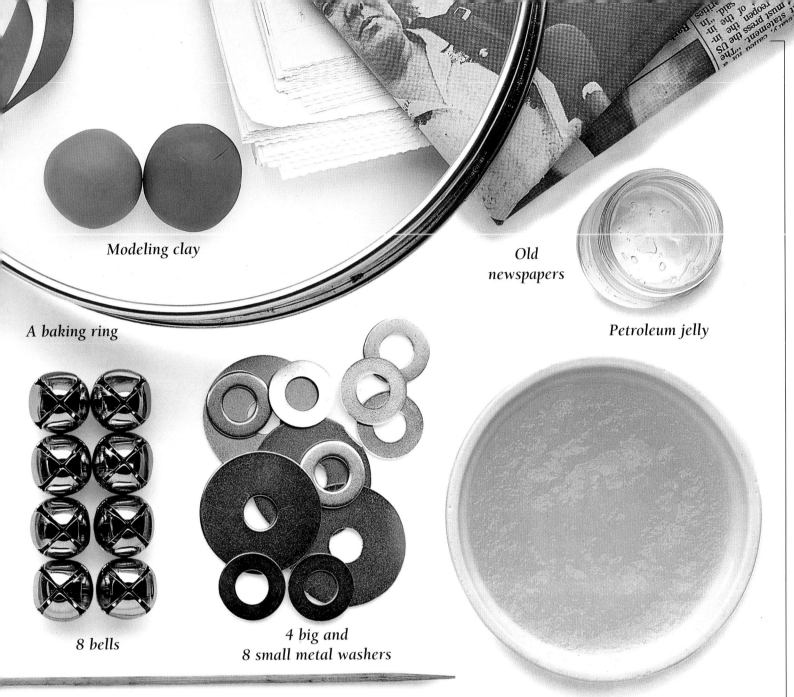

Modeling clay

Old newspapers

A baking ring

Petroleum jelly

8 bells

4 big and
8 small metal washers

Wallpaper paste*

Washer tambourine

1 Spread petroleum jelly over the ring. Press on four thick rectangles of clay as shown. Paste paper pieces around them to the ring until it is ¼ in (0.5 cm) thick.

2 When the paper is dry, peel off the clay and slide the papier-mâché off the ring. Cut the wooden skewer into four pieces.

3 Thread one big and two small washers onto each skewer piece. Stick one skewer to each opening with layers of paper.

* Ask an adult to mix the paste for you. Always wash your hands after using the paste.

15

Tambourine Jamboree

Finishing off

Cut off the rough edges around the paper rings. Stick two layers of newspaper along the trimmed edges and leave the rings to dry.

Painting tambourines

Paint the rings with poster paints. Do the outsides first and leave them to dry, then paint the insides. Glaze the rings in the same way.

Final touches

When the glaze is dry, tie bells onto the plain ring with colored thread. Then tie on lengths of colored ribbon.

And here are the finished tambourines! When the glaze has dried, the tambourines are ready to play. First, try shaking them in the air. Then hold the tambourine in one hand and tap it against the palm of your other hand in time to some music.

Washer tambourine

As you shake this tambourine, the washers rattle against each other and make a pretty jingling sound.

Washer jingles

SWALLOW TAILS

Cutting a 'V'-shape into the ends of the ribbons prevents the ribbons from fraying and looks very nice, too.

GLAZING ACT

Glazing the tambourine makes it much stronger, and protects the painted decorations against damage.

RIBBON STREAMERS
Knot two long pieces of colored ribbon around each bell.

BELL ROPE
Tie the bells onto the ring with thread the same color as the paint you have chosen.

Silver bell

Jingle bells
The bells make a bright, light, tinkling sound when you shake the tambourine. Try tying bells of two different sizes to the ring for a two-tone sound.

17

T-SHIRT PAINTING

Paint your own T-shirts and then wear your original designs! You will be amazed at how easy it is to make them. You can create a unique pattern every time by splattering one color or more onto the fabric. Always remember to lay down lots of newspaper when flicking paint in this way.

You will need special fabric paints for this project. These can be bought from arts and crafts stores. Check the instructions that come with your paints. You may need to ask an adult to iron your T-shirt on the reverse side to fix the paint when it has dried. Turn the page to see the finished splattered T-shirt. You will also find some other ideas for painting on fabric.

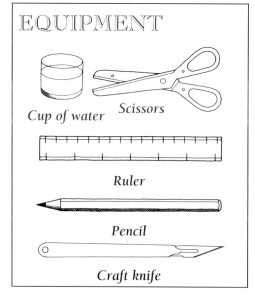

EQUIPMENT

Cup of water   *Scissors*

Ruler

Pencil

Craft knife

You will need

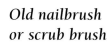

Masking tape

Fabric paints (Choose colors that will show up well on your T-shirt.)

Old nailbrush or scrub brush

T-shirt

18

Splattering the T-shirt

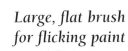

Plastic knife

Large, flat brush for flicking paint

Two sheets of corrugated cardboard (larger than T-shirt)

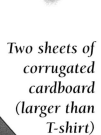

Paintbrush

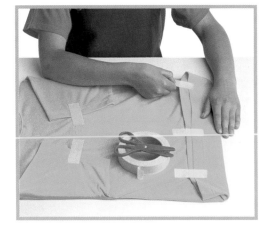

1 Push one sheet of cardboard into the shirt to stop the paint from soaking through.* Tape the sleeves and base of shirt as shown.

2 Draw a square with 8-in (20-cm) sides in the middle of the other sheet of cardboard. Ask an adult to cut out square, into frame.

3 Place the cutout square in the middle of the front of the shirt. Mark the position of the square with tape. Then remove the square.

4 Line up the frame with the tape on the T-shirt and tape it down, as shown. Cover any parts of the T-shirt that still show.

5 Put fabric paint on a nailbrush. Use a plastic knife to flick the paint away from your body onto the shirt. Leave the paint to dry.

6 Dip a large brush into a new color. Splatter the paint onto the T-shirt. When dry, ask an adult to iron the shirt to fix the paint.**

** First check the instructions that come with your paints.

* Cut cardboard to fit inside T-shirt.

19

Dazzling Designs

Here are three finished T-shirts plus some ideas for other things that you can decorate with fabric paints. Try painting a pair of socks or a baseball cap to match your T-shirt, or use your paints to brighten up old handkerchiefs, pillowcases, tablecloths, or cotton scarves. Also see pages 6 and 24 for ideas on stencils and prints.

Printed daisy

SOCKS TO MATCH

Try painting a pair of socks to match your T-shirt.

FABRIC PAINTING TIPS

• Ask an adult to iron the fabric first so that it is completely flat when you paint it.
• Always put a thick sheet of cardboard under the fabric because the paint will soak through.
• The fabric will absorb a lot of paint, so you may need two coats. Leave the first coat to dry before you paint the second.

SPLATTERED SQUARE

A little fabric paint goes a long way when splattering. Load your brush with paint and keep splattering and flicking until no more paint comes off.

SPLATTER PATTERN

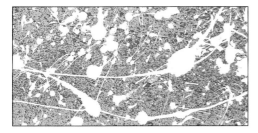

You can splatter the back of the shirt as well as the front.

When you take away the frame and masking tape, you will be left with a neat splattered square. You can use triangular or round frames to make different-shaped designs.

PRINTED DAISIES

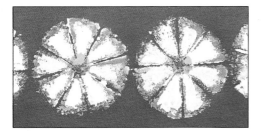

STENCILED CAR

Above are the T-shirt designs close-up.

Printed
polka dots

Stenciled
car

DOTTED HANDKERCHIEF

Turn a plain cotton handkerchief
into a polka-dotted one. A cotton
swab was used to print this pattern.

CAP

Try stenciling a
design on the
bill of a cap.

VEHICLE
STENCILS

Three stencils
have been used
on this shirt. The
white rectangles
were sponged on
first. Then the blue
car and truck were
stenciled on top.
Turn to page 6
for instructions
on stenciling.

DAISY PRINTS

Modeling clay was
used to make the printing
blocks for the daisies on
this shirt. Chains of
daisies have been printed
across the front and back
of the
T-shirt and around
the sleeves.

You can touch up
any faint prints
with a paintbrush.

21

PRINTING PRESS

Even the tiniest present looks special if it is wrapped in handmade paper. You can print your own original wrapping paper and gift tags using the simplest everyday objects, such as potatoes and leaves. Here and on the next two pages you can find out how to do potato and leaf prints, and use stencils for printing. Cover your worktable with newspaper and start your very own printing press.

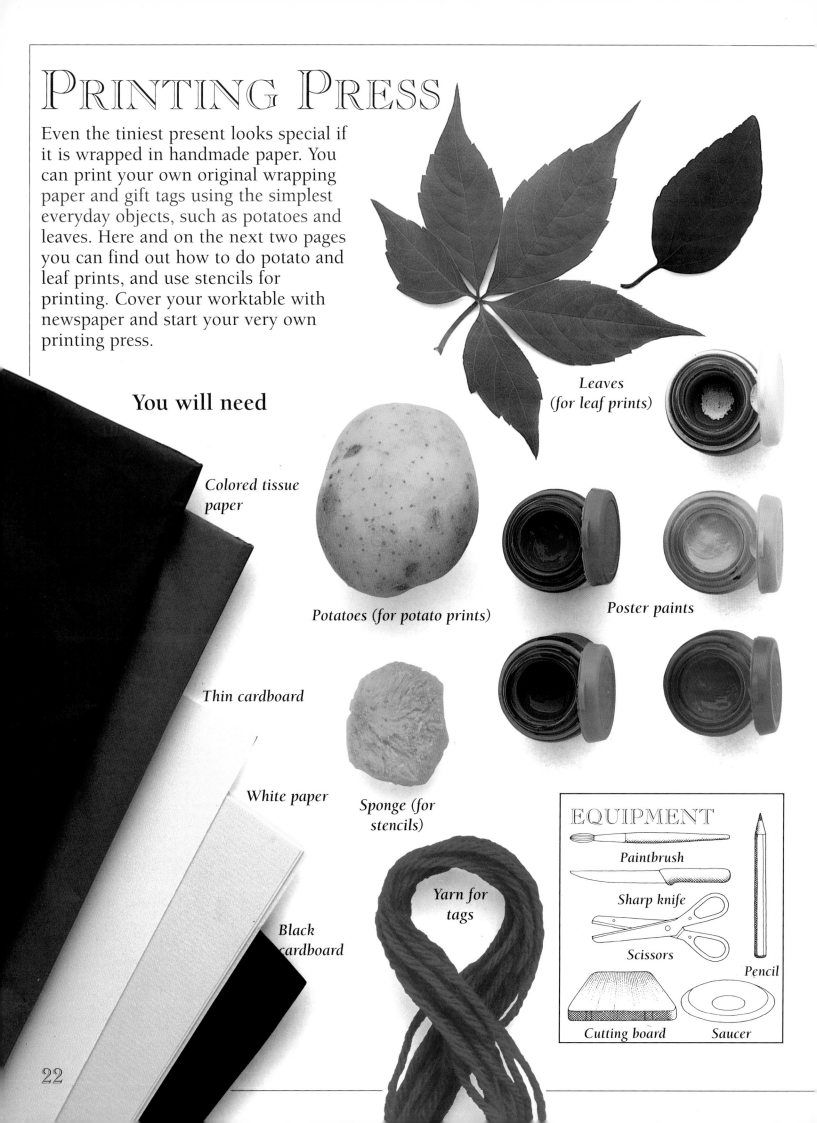

Leaves
(for leaf prints)

You will need

Colored tissue paper

Potatoes (for potato prints)

Poster paints

Thin cardboard

White paper

Sponge (for stencils)

Black cardboard

Yarn for tags

EQUIPMENT

Paintbrush

Sharp knife

Scissors

Pencil

Cutting board   Saucer

Christmas tree potato prints

1 Cut a potato in half. On one half of the potato draw a tree shape. Cut away the potato around the tree to make it stand out.*

2 Mix some green paint with a little water in a saucer. Press the cut potato into the paint, then down onto a big piece of paper.

3 Make tree prints all over the paper. Cut a pot out of the other half of the potato. Use red paint to print pots under the trees.

GIFT TAGS

For gift tags, do single prints on small pieces of cardboard. Make a hole in the corner of each one and tie a piece of yarn through it.

PRINTED PAPER

*Ask an adult to help you with this.

23

SIMPLE PRINTS

Stenciled tulip paper

1 To make a stencil, fold a piece of cardboard in half. Draw half a tulip and a leaf on one side. Cut them out and open the cardboard.

2 Mix thick poster paint in saucers. Hold the stencil flat on paper. Dab the sponge in pink paint, then over the cutout tulip.

3 Dab another piece of sponge in green paint, then over the cut-out leaves. Lift the stencil carefully off the paper.

4 Repeat the stencils to make a tulip pattern all over the paper. Use a single stencil print to make gift tags. Try different colors and other shapes, like the apple below.

Leaf prints

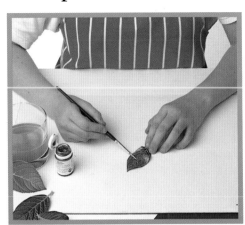  

1 Lay a fresh, non-evergreen leaf down on newspaper and paint one side of it with thick poster paint straight from the jar.

2 Lay the leaf facedown on a big piece of paper. Cover the leaf with a piece of scrap paper and rub across it with your fist.

3 Lift off the scrap paper, then the leaf. Make more prints the same way all over the paper, repainting the leaf each time.

SHINING LEAVES

Here is another idea for your painting press. Brush gold poster paint over different-shaped leaves. Print them on colored tissue paper or cardboard.

ANIMAL FRIEZE

Here you can find out how to make printing blocks by gluing string onto thick cardboard. You can use the blocks to print a frieze to go around the walls of your room. Try making a printing block of your favorite animal. Keep the string picture simple—just an outline is best.

EQUIPMENT

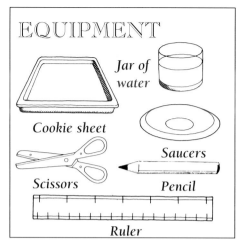

Jar of water

Cookie sheet

Saucers

Scissors

Pencil

Ruler

You will need

Thick colored paper

Thin string

Thick cardboard

A piece of thin household sponge

White glue

Leaves

Cotton swab

Paintbrush

Printing roller

*Ready-mixed, water-based paints**

* You can buy these in large squeeze bottles.

Making the blocks

1 Draw the outline of an animal on a piece of thick cardboard. You can draw any animal or trace the elephants on the next page.

2 Glue lengths of string to the outline. Use shorter lengths of string for eyes and ears. When the glue is dry, cut around the animal.

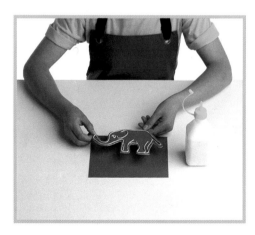

3 To finish the printing block, glue the string animal to another piece of thick cardboard as shown. Leave it to dry.

Printing the frieze

1 Put some paint in an old cookie sheet. Paint the string printing block with a printing roller or a wide paintbrush.

2 Place the block facedown on a long strip of thick paper. Press down firmly on the back of the block. Then lift it up carefully.

3 Print enough animals to fill the paper. Print a background with leaves, a sponge, a piece of cardboard, and a cotton swab.

The finished frieze

In this frieze, the trunks and tails of elephants link up to make a chain!

Red and green paints were mixed together to make brown.

Try painting the back of leaves with a brush and then printing them onto the paper.

You can use a larger or smaller animal to start and finish the frieze.

Tusks painted with a cotton swab

Grass printed with the edge of cardboard.

Branches painted with a cotton swab

Ground printed with sponge

STRING PRINTING TIPS

• Practice on scrap paper first.
• It may take a couple of coats of paint to make your string block print because the string will soak up a lot of paint.
• If there are gaps in some of your prints, fill them in with a paintbrush.

ELEPHANTS ON THE MARCH
You can make the frieze as long or as short as you want.

27

PAINTED PEBBLES

Turn pebbles into colorful painted fish and create an
amazing underwater world for them to swim in! The
pebbles hang in a shallow box on invisible thread. Look
on the beach or in a park for different-sized pebbles or
stones and fishlike shapes. Find some pictures of
tropical fish to give you ideas on how to paint them.
Turn the page to see the finished seascape.

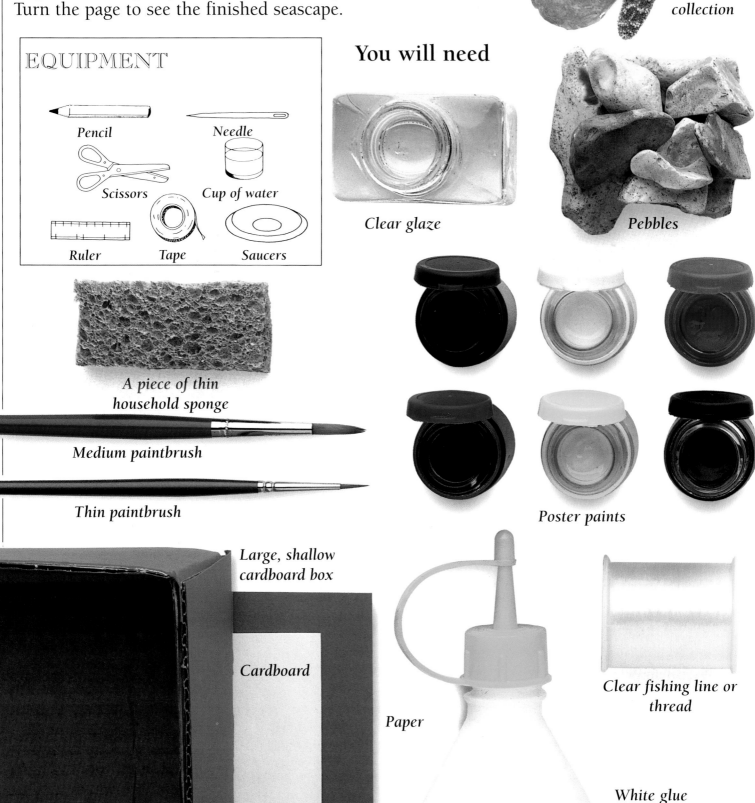

Beach
collection

EQUIPMENT

Pencil

Needle

Scissors

Cup of water

Ruler

Tape

Saucers

You will need

Clear glaze

Pebbles

A piece of thin
household sponge

Medium paintbrush

Thin paintbrush

Poster paints

Large, shallow
cardboard box

Cardboard

Paper

Clear fishing line or
thread

White glue

Making the seascape

1 Paint or glue paper over any writing on your box to give it a neat finish. You may need two coats of paint if you paint the box.

2 Paint a sandy seabed and an underwater background on the inside of the box. Try dabbing on paint with a sponge.

3 Draw sea plants and corals on cardboard and cut them out. Fold over the bottom of the plants and corals so that they stand up.

4 Paint the plants and corals with a sponge. When dry, glue along the flaps and stick them to the bottom of the box to make a scene.

5 Wash and dry the pebbles. Mix some white paint with glue and use this to paint an undercoat on the pebbles. Leave them to dry.

6 Put the pebbles on a saucer so you can turn them without touching them. Use paints mixed with glue to paint the pebbles.

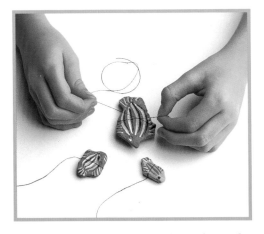

7 When the paint is dry, glaze the pebbles to protect the paint. When they are dry, tie a length of thread around each pebble.*

8 Ask an adult to use a needle to pull the fishing line through the top of the box, as shown.** Tape down the ends.

9 Arrange shells, driftwood, or stones in the base of the box. You can paint sea animals on more pebbles and add these also.

*We have used black thread to show you what to do. You should use clear fishing line or thread.
**Hold the fish in place first to decide where you want them to hang.

Fishy Scene

You can keep the finished underwater scene on a table, bookshelf, or windowsill. Use as many fish and shells as you like. If you tap the box gently, all the fish will move, just as if they are swimming in the water!

SETTING THE SCENE

Wait for everything to dry before you assemble the scene. Hang the fish at different levels so that they fill the box.

PLANTS AND CORALS

You can add depth to the scene by positioning large sea plants and corals at the back and smaller ones in the middle and at the front of the box. The fish can swim in between the plants and corals.

SCHOOLS OF FISH

Fish often swim together in groups or "schools." Here the orange, yellow, and blue fish have been arranged into groups.

In addition to fish, you can paint sea plants, crabs, or other sea creatures on stones.

Use a seaside collection of shells, stones, small rocks, or driftwood for the seabed.

You can leave some of the box showing to add texture to the scene.

The outside of the box has been covered with blue paper.

If the fishing line slips off the pebbles, use clear tape to hold it in place.

MIXING COLORS

Different shades of blue have been made for the background by mixing up different amounts of white with blue paint. The paint has been dabbed on with a sponge.

FABULOUS FISH!

The pebbles were painted in two stages. The base color was painted first. Once dry, eyes, fins, and scales were painted on top with a thin brush.

The plants and corals were painted by dabbing on orange, green, and white paint with a sponge. Try sponging one color over another.

31